DOGS

DOGS

Grange
BOOKS

A QUANTUM BOOK

Published by Grange Books
an imprint of Grange Books Plc
The Grange
Kingsnorth Industrial Estate
Hoo, nr. Rochester
Kent ME3 9ND

1-84013-128-4

This book is produced by
Quantum Books Ltd
6 Blundell Street
London N7 9BH

Project Manager: Rebecca Kingsley
Project Editor: Judith Millidge
Design/Editorial: David Manson
Andy McColm, Maggie Manson

The material in this publication previously appeared in
The Illustrated Encyclopedia of Dog Breeds,
An Introduction to Dog Care
Dog Facts

QUMSPDG
Set in Futura
Reproduced in Singapore by United Graphic Ltd
Printed in Singapore by Star Standard Industries (Pte) Ltd

Contents

MAN'S BEST FRIEND, 6
Descent of the Dog, 8
Preparing for a New Pet, 10
Providing a Proper Diet, 12
Grooming and Basic Care, 13
Breed Classification, 14

DOG BREEDS, 16
Utility Breeds, 18
Working Breeds, 24
Herding Breeds, 30
Gundogs, 36
Hounds, 44
Terriers, 50
Toy Breeds, 58

Index, 64

MAN'S BEST FRIEND

The dog is a creature that humans have never had to subdue into subservience, or with which they have been forced into battle. It appears that the dog formed an alliance with humans of its own free will, and a long-lasting partnership has developed on the basis of mutual friendship and trust.

Descent of the Dog

Before buying a dog, it is essential to get as much information as possible about all the different breeds, as this will help you select a dog that meets your requirements. This is important not only in terms of looks and size, but also character and temperament. To know the nature of your dog we first need to trace its origins.

THE FIRST DOGS

Canidae, the family of beasts of prey from which dogs, wolves, foxes and jackals are descended, first began evolving from prehistoric mammals some 60 million years ago. The dog family, *Canis familiaris*, can be traced back to the Miacis, a tree-climbing, weasel-like carnivore that lived around 50 million years ago. However the Tomarctus, a fox-like animal that appeared 35 million years later, is believed to be the true ancestor.

WOLF IN SHEEP'S CLOTHING

The Tomarctus had disappeared by the middle of the Pleistocene age, 1 million years ago, and today it is agreed that the more recent ancestor of the dog is the social wolf.

THE LEADER OF THE PACK

Many of the behaviour patterns of the domestic dog today, especially when socialising with other dogs, can be traced back to that of the wolf pack. This fact helps to explain why the domestic dog readily respects the authority of a human owner. The owner has become a substitute pack leader. The dog feels secure in the subordinate role and wants only to win the leader's approval.

All members of the species Canis familiaris *are thought to descend from wolves. Both animals are highly social and have many behavioural traits in common.*

The Miacis (left) and Tomarctus (below) are the dog's early ancestors.

Common characteristics of dogs and wolves.

- Meat-eaters
- 42 teeth
- 4 or 5 toes on fore-feet
- 4 toes on hind-feet
- Run on their toes
- Non-retractable claws
- Female 63-day gestation period
- Fairly large litters
- At birth, eyes are closed
- Live in packs
- Respect for pack leader

Preparing for a New Pet

Don't make a hasty decision about your choice of dog. After all, the dog you choose is destined to be your companion for twelve or maybe more years. Take time to select a dog that meets your requirements.

CHOOSING A DOG

Once you have decided which breed you want, you must make up your mind whether you would like a dog or a bitch. You must decide whether the dog is to be big or small and short- or long-coated. Bear in mind that a long coat requires extensive grooming and that even a short-coated breed with a light colour will deposit noticeable hairs on the carpet.

PLANNING AHEAD

Experienced dog owners, lucky enough to have big gardens, often net or fence off an area specially for their pets. This enables them to protect the remaining area for flowers, foliage and horticultural activities. However, you may wish to confine your dog to paved areas which can be easily swilled down with disinfectant.

BREEDER'S TIPS

- Check that everyone in your home really wants a dog
- Be prepared to travel some distance to get the right dog
- See the mother of the litter to get an idea of full-grown size
- Make sure the Certificate of Pedigree is in order
- Make sure the Form of Transfer is signed by the breeder
- Don't buy a dog if you are out at work all day
- Don't buy an Afghan when you really want a Yorkshire Terrier
- Don't choose a long-coated breed if you have no time for grooming

MAN'S BEST FRIEND

INDOOR KENNELS

An indoor wire kennel with a plastic removable floor tray is an excellent investment. Put the pup's bed in it, then he can sleep in the kennel and be placed in it securely when you want to leave him for short periods thus preventing chewed furniture and other destructive chaos.

Remember! Indoor kennels are a boon for house-training, as the caged pet rarely soils its own bed, but don't keep your puppy shut in for too long!

WHAT ELSE TO BUY

There are numerous types of beds and bedding, but the polyurethane type of bed is preferable. Wicker baskets tend to get chewed to pieces. Also needed will be a food bowl, soft puppy brush and a lead and collar. Finally, make sure that toys are made of durable plastic or rubber that can't be swallowed.

Remember! A puppy will soon outgrow its collar and basket so don't invest too much money until it has matured.

Providing a Proper Diet

Dogs have the same nutritional requirements as humans. They need a balanced diet containing protein, carbohydrates and fat with added vitamins and minerals. Plenty of drinking water is essential.

NUTRITIONAL SCIENCE
Scientifically prepared foods are designed to meet the nutritional requirements of the dog. They are used by most owners as much for the benefit of the dog as for convenience.

Age-related diets are available for puppies, adult dogs and senior dogs providing different levels of nutrition as the dog gets older. Hypo-allergenic and additive-free food can also be obtained for dogs with sensitive gastric systems or allergies.

Always ensure a plentiful supply of drinking water.

Dog foods come in a variety of forms.

- Meaty canned products
- Cans of complete semi-moist meat
- Complete dry dog food
- Biscuits

Try out different types of food to find which suits your dog best.

Grooming and Basic Care

Whether show dog or family pet, your dog will benefit from a daily grooming. This makes the dog look and feel good and gives the owner an opportunity to check for fleas, minor injuries or other problems.

Some breeds need considerably more grooming than others so if your time is limited it is advisable to choose a breed which does not require intricate preparation.

Discuss with the breeder the basic equipment you will require.

Routine checks when you groom your dog.

- **Ears** Check the ears and ear flaps for wax or canker. Clean gently with ear wipes. Never probe inside the ear
- **Eyes** Wipe away stains and discharges with eye swabs. Check for inflammation and opacity of cornea
- **Teeth** Clean teeth with canine toothpaste and brush. Take your dog for regular scaling to the vet
- **Nails** Carefully trim the nails every 3 months. It is probably best undertaken by the vet

Breed Classification

Dog breeds are divided into groups and these are of considerable help and importance not only in categorising the breeds for exhibition purposes, but also in aiding the purchaser to select the breed best suited to his needs.

UTILITY BREEDS
May have performed tasks in the past, but they are now companions, like the Chow Chow.

HERDING BREEDS
Originally bred to herd, they are also extremely adaptable. The German Shepherd, for example, is a well-known police dog.

WORKING BREEDS
Traditional guards and workers — rescue, sled and armed services dogs such as the Rottweiler.

GUNDOGS
Used variously to detect, flush out and retrieve game. Usually good natured, like the Golden Retriever.

MAN'S BEST FRIEND

HOUNDS

Divided into those that hunt by scent, the Beagle for instance, and those that rely on good eyesight, such as the Greyhound.

TERRIERS

Bred to go to ground, hunting vermin and bolting foxes from their lair. Terriers are affectionate by nature, like the Yorkshire Terrier.

Caring for your dog

The key boxes in each entry provide at a glance the basic requirements of each breed. One is the least needed; four the greatest required.

EXERCISE

FOOD

GROOMING

HOUSE SPACE

Many toy breeds are splendid guards, keenly intelligent and affectionate like the Pomeranian.

DOG BREEDS

Utility Breeds, 18
Working Breeds, 24
Herding Breeds, 30
Gundogs, 36
Hounds, 44
Terriers, 50
Toy Breeds, 58

BOSTON TERRIER

The Boston Terrier is a compactly built, well-balanced dog with a rather short body. It is a good companion, nevertheless it is determined and self willed. The breed takes its name from the city where it was developed as a crossbred Bulldog/Terrier.

Origin USA.
Height 38–43cm (15–17in).
Weight 7–11kg (15–25lb).
Coat Short and smooth.
Colour Brindle with white markings.
Longevity 10–12 years.
Character Lively, intelligent, loving family pet.

2	2	1	3

BULLDOG

Despite its fearsome appearance the Bulldog adores children and makes a delightful pet. Sadly, it has quite a short life span and only has a walking capacity of about half a mile. Care must be taken to avoid overexertion in hot weather.

Origin Great Britain.
Height 30–36cm (12–14in).
Weight 18–25kg (40–55lb).
Coat Short, smooth, finely textured.
Colour Tan, brindle, piebald.
Longevity 9–10 years.
Character Gentle and good natured.

1	2	1	2

U T I L I T Y   B R E E D S

FRENCH BULLDOG

Also known as the 'Frenchie', this breed usually gets on well with children and other pets. Owners must become accustomed to its gentle snuffling and occasional sulks. As with all flat-nosed breeds, exercise in hot weather should be avoided.

Origin France.
Height 30cm (12in).
Weight 11–13kg (24–28lb).
Coat Short, smooth, finely textured.
Colour Brindle, pied or fawn.
Longevity 11–12 years.
Character Good natured, affectionate, courageous.

2	2	1	2

DALMATIAN

A friendly and outgoing carriage dog capable of great speed, the Dalmatian should be free of any aggression or nervousness. It requires plenty of exercise and is highly intelligent. However, deafness in this breed is quite common.

Origin Dalmatia (Croatia).
Height 48–59cm (19–23in).
Weight 23–25kg (50–55lb).
Coat Short, dense, sleek and glossy.
Colour White with black/brown spots.
Longevity 12–14 years.
Character Affectionate and energetic.

3	2	1	3

FINNISH SPITZ

While still a favourite with hunters in Scandinavia, the Finnish Spitz is kept almost entirely as a companion and show dog elsewhere. It is good with children and adept at guarding. It requires plenty of brushing and daily exercise.

Origin Finland.
Height 39–50cm (15–20in).
Weight 11–16kg (25–35lb).
Coat Short on head, longer on body.
Colour Reddish gold.
Longevity 12–14 years.
Character Faithful and home-loving.

| 3 | 2 | 1 | 2 |

SCHNAUZER

There are three varieties, the Standard, the Giant and the Miniature. They were originally used as all-purpose farm dogs and made good ratters.

Origin Germany.
Height Standard 44–49cm (17–19in).
Giant 60–70cm (23–27in).
Miniature 30–31cm (12–14in).
Weight Standard 15 kg (33lb).
Giant 33–35kg (73–77lb).
Miniature 6–7kg (13–15lb).
Coat Harsh and wiry, soft undercoat.
Colour Pure black, or pepper and salt.
Longevity 12–14 years.
Character Robust, attractive, playful.

| 2 | 2 | 2 | 2 |

CHOW CHOW

The Chow Chow has always had a reputation for ferocity but, although a formidable opponent, it is unlikely to attack unless provoked. It makes a good pet but requires considerable grooming daily with a wire brush.

Origin China.
Height 46–56cm (18–22in).
Weight 20–32kg (45–70lb).
Coat Abundant, dense, coarse.
Colour Solid black, red, blue, fawn and cream.
Longevity 11–12 years.
Character Faithful, but strong minded.

2	2	3	2

LHASA APSO

The Lhasa Apso is a small indoor watchdog originally kept in the temples and palaces of Ancient Tibet. It is a firm family favourite and makes an excellent pet, despite having a coat that requires a great deal of grooming.

Origin Tibet.
Height 26cm (10in).
Weight 6–7kg (13–15lb).
Coat Long, heavy, straight top coat.
Colour Golden, smoke, black particolour.
Longevity 13–14 years.
Character Happy and adaptable.

1	1	2	1

SHIH TZU

The Shih Tzu whose Chinese name means 'lion dog' originates from Western China. It could be the result of crossbreeding between the Pekingese and the Lhasa Apso with which it is sometimes confused.

Origin China.
Height 23–27cm (10–11in).
Weight 4–8 kg (9–18lb).
Coat Long, dense.
Colour All colours permissible.
Longevity 13–14 years.
Character Courageous and elegant.

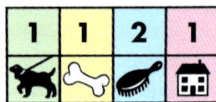

1	1	2	1

SHAR-PEI

An unusual and attractive breed, the Shar-Pei was used to herd flocks and hunt wild boar in China. It was also matched against other dogs in trials of strength. No longer the 'rarest dog in the world', it is affectionate, calm and independent.

Origin China.
Height 46–51cm (18–20in).
Weight 18–25kg (40–55lb).
Coat Short, bristly.
Colour Solid black, red, fawn, cream.
Longevity 12–14 years.
Character Alert and active.

2	2	1	2

U T I L I T Y   B R E E D S

POODLE

The Poodle's intelligence makes it popular at obedience trials as well as being a good family pet and show dog. It comes in three size varieties: the Standard Poodle, Miniature Poodle and Toy Poodle.

Origin Germany.
Height Standard 37–38cm (14–15in).
Miniature 28–38cm (11–15in).
Toy 25–28cm (10–11in).
Weight Standard 20–32kg (45–70lb).
Miniature 12–14kg (26–30lb).
Toy 6.5–7.5kg (14–16lb).
Coat Profuse, dense, harsh texture.
Colour All solid colours.
Longevity 11–15 years.
Character Dependable, happy.

2	1	3	1

BICHON FRISE

'Bichon' is French for lap dog. Similar in appearance to the Miniature Poodle the Bichon has always been bred as a pet and is recognised as a Franco-Belgian breed. It requires extensive regular grooming.

Origin Canary Islands.
Height 23–30cm (9–11in).
Weight 3–6kg (7–12lb).
Coat Long fine and corkscrew curls.
Colour White cream or apricot.
Longevity 14 years.
Character Friendly, lively, easily trained.

2	1	4	1

BOXER

The Boxer is a vibrant dog and takes a long time to grow up. They enjoy long country walks but should avoid the heat of the day in summer. The Boxer is loyal, obedient and they make good guard dogs.

Origin Germany.
Height 53–63cm (21–25in).
Weight 25–32kg (55–70lb).
Coat Short, glossy, smooth.
Colour Fawn or brindle with white markings.
Longevity 12 years.
Character Fun loving, affectionate, gentle.

3	3	1	3

ROTTWEILER

The Rottweiler has been known since the Middle Ages when it was used for boarhunting, later as a cattle drover. They are excellent guard dogs in the hands of experienced owners and with knowledgeable handling a good all round family pet.

Origin Germany.
Height 55–69cm (22—27in).
Weight 41–49kg (90–110lb).
Coat Flat and coarse, medium length.
Colour Black with tan or deep brown.
Longevity 11–12 years.
Character Courageous companion-guard.

3	3	1	4

DOBERMAN

The Doberman was developed as a guard dog in the 1880s in Germany for its stamina, courage, intelligence and tracking ability. It is now used for guarding by police forces worldwide.

Origin Germany.
Height 60–70cm (24–28in).
Weight 30–40kg (66–88lb).
Coat Smooth, thick, short and close.
Colour Solid black, brown, fawn or blue with rust markings.
Longevity 12 years.
Character Intelligent, loyal and obedient.

3	2	1	3

GREAT DANE

One of the tallest dogs in the world, a gentle giant, originally used as a wild boar hunter and bodyguard. They are easy to train and enjoy being treated as one of the family. Require regular exercise on hard ground.

Origin Germany.
Height 71–76cm (28–30in).
Weight 46–54kg (100–120lb).
Coat Sleek, short and dense.
Colour Brindle, fawn, blue, black or white with black/blue ragged patches.
Longevity 8–9 years.
Character Friendly, good natured and easy to train.

3	3	1	4

BERNESE MOUNTAIN DOG

Originally developed as a herder and guard, it is still used to pull milk carts in its native Switzerland. Popular as a show dog and a family pet needing plenty of exercise and grooming.

Origin Switzerland.
Height 58–70cm (23–28in).
Weight 40kg (88lb).
Coat Thick, long, wavy, soft, shiny.
Colour Jet black with reddish and white markings.
Longevity 10–12 years.
Character Good natured, good with children and easy to train.

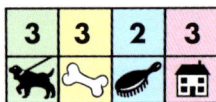

3	3	2	3

JAPANESE AKITA

The largest of the Japanese breeds, originally bred as a deer/boar hunter. It is equally happy in water or deep snow as it has webbed feet. It is revered in Japan where at one time it could only be owned by the nobility.

Origin Japan.
Height 61–71cm (24–28in).
Weight 34–49kg (75–101lb).
Coat Coarse straight outer coat, soft dense undercoat.
Colour Any color including white brindle or pinto.
Longevity 10–12 years.
Character Loyal, alert hunter, energetic.

3	2	2	3

PYRENEAN MOUNTAIN DOG

Sometimes known as the Great Pyrenees, these dogs have been used for centuries to guard flocks in the Pyrenean mountains bordering France and Spain. The dogs need plenty of exercise, grooming and must be well trained.

Origin Asia/Europe.
Height 65–81cm (26–32in).
Weight 45–60kg (99–132lb).
Coat Profuse, coarse wavy outer coat, soft thick undercoat.
Colour White, with or without patches of grey.
Longevity 11–12 years.
Character Gentle, faithful, protector.

3	3	2	3

ST BERNARD

Descended from mastiffs and famous for rescuing climbers in the Swiss Alps, the St Bernard has been revitalised by the introduction of Newfoundland blood. They require space, lots of food and gentle exercise.

Origin Switzerland.
Height 61–71cm (24–28in).
Weight 50–91kg (110–200lb).
Coat Both long and short haired breeds.
Colour Orange, mahogany-brindle, red-brindle or white.
Longevity 11 years.
Character Gentle with children, very loyal.

2	3	2	3

SAMOYED

Named after the Siberian tribe of Samoyeds, they have great endurance abilities having been taken on expeditions to the North Pole. They have also been used for hunting reindeer and as guard dogs.

Origin Siberia.
Height 46–56cm (18–22in).
Weight 23–30kg (50–66lb).
Coat Thick water resistant with a soft short undercoat.
Colour Pure white, cream; outer coat silver tipped.
Longevity 12 years.
Character Devoted, obedient.

3	2	2	2

SIBERIAN HUSKY

Developed by the Chukchi nomads of North-East Asia to pull sleds and herd reindeer, they became famous in the gold rush era of Alaska, as sled racing dogs. Since the Second World War, they have been used as search and rescue dogs.

Origin Siberia
Height 51–60cm (20–24in).
Weight 16–27kg (30–60lb).
Coat Straight, medium length, soft, dense undercoat.
Colour All colours and markings.
Longevity 11–13 years.
Character Intelligent, friendly, hard working.

4	3	2	3

MASTIFF

One of the most ancient breeds of dog, it has been used as a formidable guard dog and as a hunter. St Bernard blood was introduced in the 19th century. They are large dogs which are expensive to feed and require regular walking to build up their muscles.

Origin Turkey.
Height 70–76cm (27–30in).
Weight 86–100kg (190–220lb).
Coat Short, smooth, dense.
Colour Fawn, brindle or red.
Longevity 7–10 years.
Character Loyal, good-natured.

4	4	1	4

BULLMASTIFF

The result of a cross between the Mastiff 60% and the British Bulldog 40%, 200-300 years ago. Powerful animals, they have a large appetite, require regular exercise and need grooming every few days. Dependable with children.

Origin Great Britain.
Height 64–69cm (25–27in).
Weight 41–59kg (90–130lb).
Coat Short smooth and dense.
Colour Any shade of brindle, fawn or red; black muzzle.
Longevity 10–12 years.
Character Loyal, playful, excellent guard.

3	4	1	4

NEWFOUNDLAND

Believed to be descended from the Tibetan
Mastiff, the Newfoundland has adapted to
the conditions in Eastern Canada by devel-
oping webbed feet and an oily coat.
This allows it to remain in water for
long periods and helps its strong
rescue instinct.

Origin Canada.
Height 66–71cm (26–28in).
Weight 50–68kg (110—50lb).
Coat Double coat, dense, coarse and
oily.
Colour Black brown, grey or Landseer.
Longevity 12 years.
Character Docile, patient, very gentle.

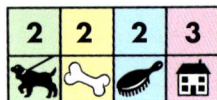

BEARDED COLLIE

One of the oldest herding dogs in
Scotland, descended from three Polish
Lowland Sheepdogs in 1514. Nearly
extinct in the 1940s, today's dogs are
the descendants of a pair bred in
Ayrshire, Scotland by Mrs G. Wilson.

Origin Poland.
Height 51–56cm (20–22in).
Weight 18–27kg (40–60lb).
Coat Flat, harsh, shaggy and slightly
wavy.
Colour Slate grey, reddish fawn with or
without white markings.
Longevity 12–13 years.
Character Alert, active, good natured.

BORDER COLLIE

Descended from the working collies on the borders of Scotland and England. Naturally good at herding with stamina and intelligence, they are used all over the world as sheepdogs.

Origin Great Britain.
Height 46–54cm (18–21in).
Weight 14–22kg (30–49lb).
Coat Either smooth or long, both are thick and straight.
Colour Variety of colour but white should not predominate.
Longevity 12–14 years.
Character Loyal, obedient, intelligent.

4	2	1	2

SHETLAND SHEEPDOG

Originally from the Shetland Islands off the North coast of Scotland where it is known as the 'Sheltie'. Believed to be descended from working collies which arrived at the islands on whaling ships.

Origin Great Britain.
Height 35–37cm (14–15in).
Weight 6–7kg (14–16lb).
Coat Long harsh outercoat, soft close undercoat.
Colour Sable, tricolour, blue merle, black and tan, black and white.
Longevity 12–14 years.
Character Sensitive, intelligent, good show and obedience dog.

2	2	2	2

OLD ENGLISH SHEEPDOG

Believed to have developed from a cross of a Briard and the Russian Owtcharka, they have been used as a drover's dog. Their docked tails were an identification mark in the 18th century when drover's dogs were exempt from taxes and they acquired the nickname of 'Bobtail'.

Origin Great Britain.
Height 53–56cm (21–22in).
Weight 30kg (66lb).
Coat Profuse, shaggy, good texture.
Colour Shades of grey, grizzle or blue.
Longevity 12–13 years.
Character Good temperament, exuberant, thrives on affection.

3	3	2	3

ROUGH COLLIE

Recognised as the star of the 'Lassie' films. They have been used as sheepdogs in the Scottish Highlands for centuries. They are intelligent and need lots of exercise. There is an identical Smooth-Haired variety.

Origin Iceland.
Height 51–65cm (20–26in).
Weight 18–34kg (40–75lb).
Coat Dense harsh outer coat.
Colour Sable and white, tricolour.
Longevity 12–13 years.
Character Loyal, affectionate, excellent guard dog.

3	3	2	3

WELSH CORGI

There are two types, Pembroke (pictured) and the Cardigan. Originally bred as herding dogs, especially for cattle where they nipped their ankles to control their movements.

Origin Great Britain.
Height 25–32cm (10–12.5in).
Weight Pembroke 11–12kg (25–27lb).
Cardigan 11–17kg (25–38lb).
Coat Pembroke. Medium and straight.
Cardigan. Short or medium.
Colour Pembroke. Red, sable, fawn.
Cardigan. Any; no white predominate.
Longevity 12–14 years.
Character Working, excellent guard.

2	2	1	2

BRIARD

One of France's most popular companion dogs. Best known as a sheepdog, having been introduced to Europe with other sheepdogs from Hungary and Russia.

Origin Asia.
Height 55–68cm (22–27in).
Weight 34kg (75lb).
Coat Long and wavy, dense undercoat.
Colour Solid black, fawn.
Longevity 11–13 years.
Character Gentle, intelligent, very energetic.

3	3	2	3

GERMAN SHEPHERD DOG

Believed to be descended from the Bronze Age wolf, they are extremely intelligent and trainable. They make excellent guide dogs for the blind as well as police dogs. They need plenty of exercise and a job to do so they do not get bored.

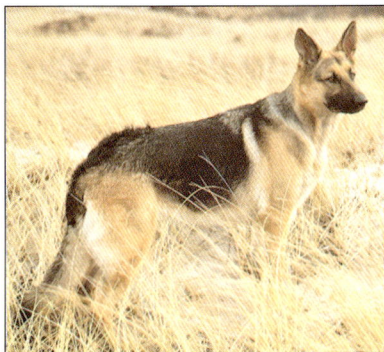

Origin Germany.
Height 55–66cm (22–26in).
Weight 34–43kg (75–95lb).
Coat Medium length, straight.
Colour Solid black or grey, with tan or grey markings.
Longevity 12–13 years.
Character Very intelligent, trainable and good guard dog.

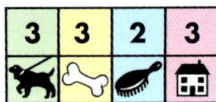

3	3	2	3

BELGIAN SHEPHERD DOG

There are four varieties: the Groenendael (pictured), the Tervueren, the Malinois and the Laekenois. All were developed from sheepdogs of different colours and sizes in Belgium at the end of the 19th century.

Origin Belgium.
Height 56–66cm (22–26in).
Weight 28kg (62lb).
Coat Either long straight or short harsh.
Colour Black, grey, red, fawn.
Longevity 12–14 years.
Character Strong herding and guarding instincts.

3	2	2	3

PICARDY SHEPHERD DOG

This breed is said to be the oldest French herding dog and is unsurpassed at guarding both flocks of sheep and herds of cattle. Trustworthy with children, they superbly combine the role of working dog and family pet.

Origin France.
Height 56–66cm (22–26in).
Weight 22–32kg (50–70lb).
Coat Hard, long with a heavy under-coat.
Colour All shades of grey and fawn.
Longevity 10–12 years.
Character Energetic, affectionate, trustworthy.

3	3	1	3

HUNGARIAN PULI

The best known of the Hungarian sheepdogs introduced by the Magyars over 1000 years ago. They have been used for herding sheep for centuries and recently for police work. Their corded coat, requires special care and attention.

Origin Hungary.
Height 37–44cm (14–18in).
Weight 10–15kg (22–33lb).
Coat Dense, corded.
Colour Black, white or grey and apricot.
Longevity 12–13 years.
Character Loyal, devoted, intelligent.

3	2	3	3

LABRADOR RETRIEVER

Introduced to Great Britain by Newfoundland fishermen who used the dogs to help land the fishing nets. Black was their usual colour although today yellow labradors are much more popular and are used as guide dogs and gundogs.

Origin Newfoundland.
Height 54–61cm (21–25in).
Weight 25–34kg (55–75lb).
Coat Short, dense, weather resistant.
Colour Solid black, yellow or liver/chocolate.
Longevity 12–14 years.
Character Easy to train, good with children, loves water.

3	2	2	3

GOLDEN RETRIEVER

Popular as a show and working dog, they were originally bred for finding, picking up and carrying hares or birds. They have developed from a combination of yellow flat coated dogs with Tweed Water Spaniels. Ideal as guide dogs for the blind.

Origin Great Britain.
Height 51–61cm (20–24in).
Weight 25–34kg (55–75lb).
Coat Flat or wavy with good feathering.
Colour Any shade of gold or cream.
Longevity 13–15 years.
Character Friendly, good family pet, sound temperament.

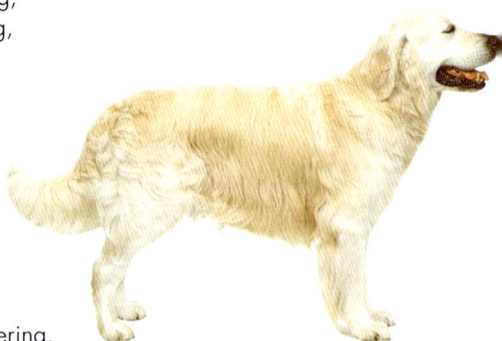

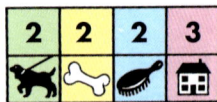

2	2	2	3

FLAT COATED RETRIEVER

Originally called the Wavy-coat Retriever, this breed is not so well known although they were very popular with gamekeepers at the turn of the century. Excellent retrievers both on land and water.

Origin Great Britain.
Height 56–61cm (22–24in).
Weight 25–35kg (55–80lb).
Coat Dense, medium length, lying flat.
Colour Solid black or solid liver.
Longevity 12–14 years.
Character Intelligent, good temperament, hardy, happiest at work.

3	2	1	3

IRISH WATER SPANIEL

An enchanting-looking animal, the Irish Water Spaniel is a first class water dog, skilled at wild fowling and trainable as an all round sporting dog. It is the tallest of the spaniels and there is a smaller American variety.

Origin Ireland.
Height 51–60cm (20–24in).
Weight 20–30kg (45–65lb).
Coat Tight dense ringlets.
Colour Dark liver with purplish tint.
Longevity 12–14 years.
Character Devoted, affectionate, boisterous.

3	2	2	3

AMERICAN COCKER SPANIEL

The breed originates from a British bitch brought back to America in the 1880s. They are the smallest of the American gundogs and until recently were shown exclusively in the ring. Latterly field trials have been reintroduced.

Origin USA.
Height 34–39cm (13–15in).
Weight 11–12kg (24–28lb).
Coat Short on head, medium on body.
Colour Black, black/brown and tan, tricolours.
Longevity 13–14 years.
Character Gundog, show dog, good with children.

2	2	3	2

CLUMBER SPANIEL

The heaviest of the spaniels, the Clumber is a slow-but-sure dog, common in the country where it excels at flushing out game over rough ground. Brought to Britain from France prior to the Revolution, to stay at Clumber Park from where they get their name.

Origin France.
Height 42–50cm (17–20in).
Weight 25–38kg (55–70lb).
Coat Abundant and silky.
Colour White with orange/lemon markings.
Longevity 12–13 years.
Character Good temperament, good family dog but ideal gundog.

2	2	2	2

GUNDOGS

ENGLISH COCKER SPANIEL

Originally from Spain, the Cocker is the smallest of the spaniel gundogs and gets its name from being used at flushing out woodcocks. They are first class gundogs, as well as gentle pets. Special care should be given to their distinctive long ears.

Origin Spain.
Height 38–43cm (15–17in).
Weight 13–15kg (28–32lb).
Coat Flat and silky texture.
Colour Various and pure colours.
Longevity 13–14 years.
Character Gentle, first-class gundog, popular pet.

ENGLISH SPRINGER SPANIEL

Once known as the Norfolk Spaniel, the breed were used for springing or flushing out game prior to shotguns being used. They are popular gundogs with unlimited stamina and love water.

Origin Great Britain.
Height 48–51cm (19–20in).
Weight 22–25kg (49–55lb).
Coat Close and straight.
Colour Liver/white, black/white, with tan.
Longevity 12–14 years.
Character Intelligent, reliable, good with children.

WELSH SPRINGER SPANIEL

Smaller than the English Spaniel,
the Welsh Spaniels are excellent
retrievers with lots of stamina
and are superb working dogs. They
have a distinctive rich, red and white
coat which distinguishes them from
other spaniels.

Origin Great Britain.
Height 42–48cm (17–19in).
Weight 16–20kg (35–45lb).
Coat Straight and flat, silky.
Colour Rich red and white only.
Longevity 12–14 years.
Character Hardworking, affectionate.

3	2	2	2

IRISH SETTER

The breed was developed through
crossing the Irish Water Spaniel, the
Spanish Pointer and English and
Gordon Setters. It is ideally suited for
work as a gundog in open countryside
and is famed for its classic stance.

Origin Ireland.
Height 63–69cm (25–27in).
Weight 27–32kg (60–70lb).
Coat Short on head and legs;
moderately long on body.
Colour Rich chestnut.
Longevity 13 years.
Character Good family pet,
boundless energy.

3	2	1	3

GUNDOGS

40

IRISH RED AND WHITE SETTER

They are said to be evolved from red and white spaniels brought to Ireland from France and crossed with Pointers. Combination of sportsman's dog and family pet.

Origin Ireland.
Height 59–67cm (23–27in).
Weight 18–32kg (40–70lb).
Coat Flat, straight with good feathering.
Colour Particoloured, white base with red patches.
Longevity 13 years.
Character Good natured, affectionate.

3	2	1	

GORDON SETTER

Scotland's only native gundog, formerly known as the Gordon Castle Setter. The largest of the setters is at its best when hunting game birds particularly grouse. They are able to work without water for longer periods than most other setters.

Origin Great Britain.
Height 57–70cm (23–26in).
Weight 20–36kg (45–80lb).
Coat Short on head/legs; long on body.
Colour Deep, shining coal-black with tan markings.
Longevity 13 years.
Character Good family pet, tireless gundog, good watchdog.

3	3	1	3

ENGLISH SETTER

The oldest of the setters, they were developed to hunt in open country. Beautiful and affectionate, the breed successfully combines the role of family pet and sportsman's dog.

Origin Great Britain.
Height 60–68cm (24–27in).
Weight 18–32kg (40–70lb).
Coat Long, straight and dense.
Colour Black/white, orange/white liver/white.
Longevity 14 years.
Character Good natured, friendly, loyal and affectionate.

3	2	1	3

POINTER

Thought to have originated in Spain, the Pointer is famed for its classic stance. They are popular as show dogs but were originally used as gundogs, when they would 'point' to where game was lurking. Good with children.

Origin Spain.
Height 57–70cm (23–28in).
Weight 20–34kg (45–75lb).
Coat Short, dense and smooth.
Colour Orange/white, liver/white, black/white.
Longevity 13–14 years.
Character Affectionate, easy to train.

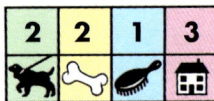

2	2	1	3

MÜNSTERLÄNDER (Large and Small)

The breed combines the best qualities of the setter and the spaniel and has been established as a gundog in Germany since the 18th century. The Small Münsterländer is the result of crossbreeding the Brittany and German Long-haired Pointer.

Origin Germany.
Height Large 58–61cm (23–24in). Small 47–55cm (19–22in).
Weight Large 25–29kg (55–65lb). Small 15kg (33lb).
Coat Long, dense with feathering.
Colour Black head, body white or blue roan. Small liver and white ticking.
Longevity 12–13 years.
Character Loyal, friendly, trustworthy.

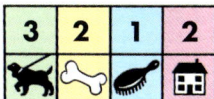

3	2	1	2

WEIMERANER

They are believed to have developed from the crossing of Bloodhounds with local pointers and hunting dogs. Once used against big game, they are now popular as police dogs where their intelligence and agility are put to good use.

Origin Germany.
Height 56–69cm (22–27in).
Weight 32–38kg (70–85lb).
Coat Short, smooth and sleek.
Colour Metallic silver grey.
Longevity 12–13 years.
Character Intelligent. Makes a good pet if given enough exercise.

3	2	1	3

AFGHAN HOUND

They are an ancient breed of dog and a member of the greyhound family. Their long shaggy coat was developed to withstand the harsh climate of Afghanistan. Its speed and stamina were used to hunt leopards, wolves and jackals.

Origin Afghanistan.
Height 63–68cm (25–27in).
Weight 23–27kg (50–60lb).
Coat Long and fine.
Colour All colours acceptable.
Longevity 12–14 years.
Character Elegant, beautiful, affectionate. Slightly aloof.

3	3	3	3

BASENJI

The breed comes from Central Africa where they were used as a hunting dog They are famed for the fact that they do not bark but instead give out a kind of yodel. The Basenji wash themselves like a cat and have no doggie smell.

Origin Central Africa.
Height 40–43cm (16–17in).
Weight 10–11kg (22–24lb).
Coat Short, sleek, close and fine.
Colour Black, red, or black and tan; white chest, feet and tail tips.
Longevity 12 years.
Character Intelligent, playful, dislikes wet weather.

2	2	1	2

BLOODHOUND

They are one of the oldest hound breeds, said to have been brought to Britain by William the Conqueror in 1066. The Bloodhound has the keenest sense of smell of any domestic animal and are used to track lost people and animals.

Origin France.
Height 58–67cm (23–27in).
Weight 36–45kg (80—100lb).
Coat Smooth, short and weatherproof.
Colour Black and tan, liver and tan or red.
Longevity 10–12 years.
Character Affectionate, good with children.

4	3	1	3

BORZOI

This breed was used in Russia for wolf hunting and coursing. The dog tracked the wolf, grabbing it by the neck and throwing it so that it could be finished off by a blow from a dagger. Its in-built hunting instincts mean that it is not good with children.

Origin Russia.
Height 68–74cm (27–29in).
Weight 27–48kg (60–105lb).
Coat Silky, flat and wavy or curly.
Colour Any colour acceptable.
Longevity 11–13 years.
Character Elegant, intelligent.

3	3	1	4

BASSET HOUND

The Basset was bred from the French Basset Artésien Normand and crossed with the Bloodhound, to produce a slow-but sure dog used to track rabbits and hare. Now, kept as a companion, pet or show dog. It needs a lot of exercise.

Origin France.
Height 33–35cm (13–14in).
Weight 18–27kg (40–60lb).
Coat Hard, smooth, short and dense.
Colour Black, white/tan, lemon/ white.
Longevity 12 years.
Character Lovable, gets on well with children.

3	2	1	2

BEAGLE

The smallest of the hounds, the Beagle has been used for hunting hare and wild rabbit, and can be trained to seek out and retrieve. It is a fine show dog and needs only an average amount of exercise.

Origin Great Britain.
Height USA 33–37cm (13–15in).
UK 33–40cm (13–16in).
Weight 8–14kg (18–30lb).
Coat Short, dense and weatherproof.
Colour Any recognized hound colour.
Longevity 13 years.
Character Friendly, good with children, fine show dog.

2	2	1	2

H O U N D S

BASSET GRIFFON VENDÉEN

This breed comes in three sizes, Grand, Bassett or Petit. They are French sporting dogs. The Grand was originally used to hunt wolves and wild boar and other varieties hunt hare and rabbit.

Origin France.
Height Grand 61–66cm (24–26in).
Basset 38–43cm (15–17in).
Petit 34–38cm (13–15in).
Weight Grand 30–35kg (66–77lb).
Basset 18–20kg (40–44lb).
Petit 11–16kg (25–35lb).
Coat Rough, long and harsh.
Colour Solid fawn or hare.
Longevity 12 years.
Character Intelligent, hunters.

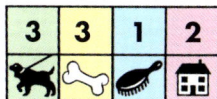

3	3	1	2

ENGLISH FOXHOUND

The breed is descended from St Hubert Hounds and the Talbot and their prime function is to hunt foxes alongside mounted huntsmen. They are able to work for long periods without a break. They cannot be kept as pets in Britain but are the property of the hunting packs.

Origin Great Britain.
Height 50–62cm (21–25in).
Weight 29–31kg (65–70lb).
Coat Short and hard.
Colour Black, white and tan, or tan and white.
Longevity 11 years.
Character Intelligent, working dog.

4	3	1	3

H O U N D S

DACHSHUND

There are six breeds of Dachshund: Smooth-haired, Long-haired and Wire-haired each occurring as both Standard and Miniature. They are derived from the oldest breeds of German hunting dogs and were bred to go to ground.

Origin Germany.
Height 13–25cm (5–10in).
Weight Standard UK 9–12kg (20–26lb); Standard US 7–14kg (16–32lb). Miniature UK about 4.5kg (10lb); Miniature US under 5kg (11lb).
Coat Smooth-haired. Dense and short. Long-haired. Soft and straight. Wire-haired. Short, straight and harsh.
Colour Any colour but white permissible.
Longevity 14–17 years.
Character Devoted pet, good watchdog.

2	2	1	1

GREYHOUND

The breed has altered little from dogs depicted on the tombs of the pharaohs and is mentioned in the Holy Bible. They were a favourite with the nobility as they were highly valued as a courser. More recently they have competed on the greyhound racing tracks.

Origin Egypt.
Height 68–76cm (27–30in).
Weight 27–32kg (60–70lb).
Coat Fine and close.
Colour Black, white, red, blue, fawn and fallow brindle.
Longevity 10–12 years.
Character Gentle, good with children, faithful, loves to chase.

3	2	1	3

WHIPPET

Resembling a small greyhound, the Whippet was bred expressly as a racing dog and is the fastest breed in the world. Adaptable to domestic life, the Whippet needs plenty of exercise.

Origin Great Britain.
Height 44–51cm (17.5–20in).
Weight 12.5kg (28lb).
Coat Short, fine and close.
Colour Any colour or mixture of colours.
Longevity 13–14 years.
Character Gentle, good with children, a fine watchdog.

3	2	1	2

IRISH WOLFHOUND

The tallest dog in the world, and the national dog of Ireland. Bred to kill wolves, they became highly prized dogs and were exported to Europe. Needs no more than average exercise.

Origin Ireland.
Height 75–85cm (30–34in).
Weight 48–55kg (105–120lb).
Coat Rough and harsh.
Colour Grey, brindle, red, black, white, fawn or wheaten.
Longevity 11 years.
Character Calm temperament, popular show dog.

3	4	1	4

BULL TERRIER

The Bull Terrier began life as a fighting dog, the result of crossing an Old English Bulldog with a terrier and is described as 'the gladiator of the canine race'. Despite its fierce appearance, it makes a faithful and devoted pet. The bitch is utterly reliable with children.

Origin Great Britain.
Height 52–55cm (21–22in).
Weight 23–28kg (52–62lb).
Coat Short and flat.
Colour White, brindle.
Longevity 11–13 years.
Character Faithful and devoted.

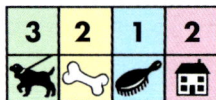

3	2	1	2

STAFFORDSHIRE BULL TERRIER

Not to be confused with the American Staffordshire Terrier or Pit Bull. Derived from a crossing of an Old English Bulldog and a terrier at a time when dog fighting and bull-baiting were popular sports. A popular pet and show dog, it adores children but does enjoy a scrap with other dogs.

Origin Great Britain.
Height 33–40cm (14–16in).
Weight 11–17kg (24–38lb).
Coat Short, smooth and dense.
Colour Red, fawn, white, black, brindle.
Longevity 11–12 years.
Character Courageous, intelligent.

2	2	1	2

AIREDALE TERRIER

The king of the terriers and the largest member of the terrier group. An expert ratter and duck-catcher, they can be trained to the gun and make good guard dogs.

Origin Great Britain.
Height 56–61cm (22–24in).
Weight 20kg (44lb).
Coat Hard, dense and wiry.
Colour Black or grizzle with tan legs and head.
Longevity 13 years.
Character Good family pet, loyal.

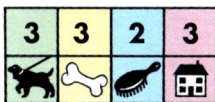

3	3	2	3

FOX TERRIER

Originally used as a stable dog hunting out vermin, they are great rabbiters and will pursue foxes as their names suggest. There are two types: smooth- and wire-haired. Needs regular grooming.

Origin Great Britain.
Height 38–39cm (15in).
Weight 7–8kg (16–18lb).
Coat Smooth. Straight, flat and smooth; Wire. Dense and very wiry.
Colour Smooth. White with tan/black. Wire. White predominates, black or tan markings.
Longevity 13–14 years.
Character Affectionate, trainable.

3	2	3	2

KERRY BLUE TERRIER

An excellent sporting dog and fine swimmer, the Kerry Blue was used to hunt badgers, foxes and otters. They are now mainly kept as pets. It has a fierce temper with other dogs or pets but is good with children.

Origin Ireland.
Height 44–49cm (17–20in).
Weight 15–18kg (33–40lb).
Coat Soft, spiky, wavy and plentiful.
Colour Blue, with or without black points.
Longevity 14 years.
Character Good guard dog.

| 2 | 2 | 2 | 2 |

PARSON JACK RUSSELL TERRIER

Named after the Parson who developed this strain of terrier from early types of wire-haired fox terriers. The intention was to produce a dog which would run with hounds and bolt the fox.

Origin Great Britain.
Height 30–35cm (12–14in).
Weight 4.5kg (10lb).
Coat Smooth, or rough and broken.
Colour Entirely white or with tan, lemon or black markings.
Longevity 10–12 years.
Character Good working dog, popular household pet, excitable.

| 3 | 2 | 1 | 2 |

T E R R I E R S

BORDER TERRIER

This dog originates from the Borders region between England and Scotland and was bred to run with hounds and to bolt the fox from its lair. The smallest of the working terriers, they make first class pets and love children.

Origin Great Britain.
Height 25cm (10in).
Weight 5–7kg (10–15lb).
Coat Harsh and dense, close undercoat.
Colour Red, wheaten, grizzle and tan, blue and tan.
Longevity 13–14 years.
Character Able to walk owners off their feet, good watchdog.

CAIRN TERRIER

Popular Scottish terriers used to catch vermin, they are named after the cairns of stones where their prey hid. Originated in the West Highlands, the Cairn is a predominantly working dog.

Origin Great Britain.
Height 24–30cm (9.5–12in).
Weight 6.0–7.5kg (13–16lb).
Coat Profuse, harsh.
Colour Cream, wheaten, red, grey or nearly black.
Longevity 14 years.
Character Affectionate, lively, adaptable, minimum grooming.

NORFOLK TERRIER

Once classified as the Norwich Terrier, the Norfolk Terrier is distinguished by its ears which drop forward. The breed is probably a mixture of Cairn, Border and Irish terriers and they are among the smallest of the terriers.

Origin Great Britain.
Height 25.5cm (10in).
Weight 5.0–5.5kg (11–12lb).
Coat Hard, wiry and straight.
Colour Red, wheaten, black and tan, or grizzle.
Longevity 14 years.
Character Sociable, hardy, alert, fearless, good temperament.

3	2	1	2

NORWICH TERRIER

The breed is named after the city of Norwich and appears to have originated in East Anglia. At one time they were classified together with the Norfolk Terrier but the breeds were separated in 1979, the Norwich having prick-up ears, the Norfolk having flat ears.

Origin Great Britain.
Height 25.5cm (10in).
Weight 4.5–5.5kg (10–12lb).
Coat Hard, wiry and straight.
Colour Red, wheaten, black and tan.
Longevity 14 years.
Character Hardy, adaptable.

3	2	1	2

SCOTTISH TERRIER

Once known as the Aberdeen Terrier, the breed was developed to dispel vermin and has taken many forms over the centuries. They have erect ears and prominent eyebrows on a long face which give the 'Scottie' a somewhat stern appearance.

Origin Great Britain.
Height 25–28cm (11in).
Weight 8–11kg (19–23lb).
Coat Sharp, dense and wiry.
Colour Black, wheaten or brindle.
Longevity 13–14 years.
Character Reliable temperament, very loyal.

2	2	1	2

WEST HIGHLAND WHITE TERRIER

Like other small working Scottish terriers, the 'Westie' was bred to hunt vermin. Their name has evolved over the years as their classification has changed. They need regular grooming to keep their coat in shape and are good with children.

Origin Great Britain.
Height 25–27cm (11in).
Weight 7–10kg (15–22lb).
Coat Harsh, and free from curl.
Colour White.
Longevity 14 years.
Character Easy to train.

2	2	3	2

SKYE TERRIER

The breed was developed from small dogs kept to go to ground after badgers, fox, otter and rabbit. Believed to originate from the Isle of Skye, and at one time thought to be the same breed as the Cairn Terrier. Its magnificent coat requires regular grooming.

Origin Great Britain.
Height 24–25cm (9–10in).
Weight 11kg (25lb).
Coat Long hard straight, flat and free from curl, with close woolly undercoat.
Colour Black, dark or light grey, fawn.
Longevity 13 years.
Character Suspicious of people.

2	2	3	2

MANCHESTER TERRIER

Once known as the Black and Tan Terrier, the Manchester Terriers have been long established as sporting terriers. The introduction of other blood such as the Doberman and the Italian Greyhound account for its smooth coat and slightly arched back.

Origin Great Britain.
Height 38–40cm (15–16in).
Weight 5–10kg (12–22lb).
Coat Close, smooth, short and glossy.
Colour Jet black and rich tan.
Longevity 13–14 years.
Character A one person animal.

2	2	1	2

DANDI DINMONT TERRIER

Believed to be a relative of the Skye
Terrier, they were originally bred to hunt
badgers and foxes. Believed to be
named after a character in a Walter
Scott novel, as the author kept these
dogs himself. Enjoys exercise and is
good with children.

Origin Great Britain.
Height 20–27cm (8–11in).
Weight 8–11kg (18–24lb).
Coat Soft, linty undercoat.
Colour Pepper or mustard.
Longevity 13–14 years.
Character Enjoys being sole
family pet.

2	2	1	2

SEALYHAM TERRIER

The breed has been traced back to the
15th century and were used to dig
badgers and hunt with hounds. The
name comes from the village of
Sealyham in Wales where they
were bred.

Origin Great Britain.
Height 31cm (12in).
Weight 8–9kg (18–20lb).
Coat Long, hard and wiry.
Colour White with lemon, brown,
blue markings.
Longevity 14 years.
Character A fine show dog and
family pet.

2	1	3	2

MALTESE

A member of the Bichon family, the Maltese is one of the oldest European breeds of lap dog. They have been painted by many famous artists such as Goya and Rubens. They are a long lived little dog and require daily grooming.

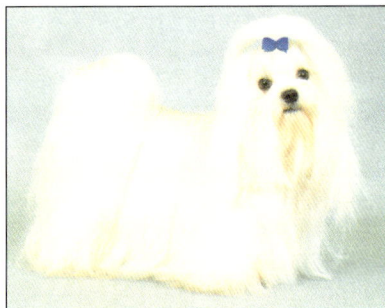

Origin Great Britain.
Height 25.5cm (10in).
Weight 2–3kg (4–7lb).
Coat Long, straight silky coat.
Colour White with lemon markings.
Longevity 14–15 years.
Character Happy, lovable, adaptable.

BRUSSELS GRIFFON (and PETIT BRABANCON)

Bred to kill vermin in stables, the rough coated Brussels Griffon became a companion dog because of its appealing character. The Petit Brabancon is believed to have had Pug, Yorkshire and Irish Terrier blood introduced into the breed which has produced a smooth coat.

Origin Belgium.
Height 18–20cm (7–8in).
Weight 2–5kg (5–11lb).
Coat Brussels Griffon. Harsh and wiry. Petit Brabancon. Soft and smooth.
Colour Red, black or black and rich tan with white markings.
Longevity 12–14 years.
Character Intelligent, cheerful.

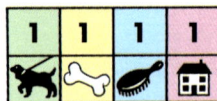

YORKSHIRE TERRIER

Developed through a crossing of the Skye and extinct Black and Tan Terriers. The 'Yorkie' is now one of the most popular toy breeds in the world. They are suited to town or country living and are utterly fearless. They are first class show dogs for those with time for intricate grooming.

Origin Great Britain.
Height 22cm (9in).
Weight 3kg (7lb).
Coat Glossy, fine and silky.
Colour Dark steel blue with rich tan.
Longevity 14 years.
Character Affectionate, bossy, lively.

2	1	4	1

PUG

It is believed to have originated in China and may be a relative of the Tibetan Mastiff. The Pug was introduced into Holland from trading ships and subsequently brought into Britain by William of Orange. They are sturdy dogs despite their small size.

Origin China.
Height 25–27cm (10–12in).
Weight 6–8kg (14–18lb).
Coat Fine, smooth, short, glossy.
Colour Silver, apricot, fawn or black.
Longevity 13–15 years.
Character Intelligent, happy.

1	1	1	1

PAPILLON

The Papillon is named after the French for butterfly and comes from the breed's erect ears. It is also known as the Continental Toy Spaniel and is often mistaken for the Long-coated Chihuahua, a variety it helped to produce.

Origin Spain.
Height 20–28cm (8–11in).
Weight 4.0–4.5kg (9–10lb).
Coat Long, abundant, silky.
Colour White with patches of any colour except liver.
Longevity 13–15 years.
Character Intelligent, obedient.

POMERANIAN

A member of the Spitz family, the Pomeranian originates from White Spitz, in Pomerania, Northern Germany, which were much larger dogs. They were bred down after being introduced to Britain about 100 years ago.

Origin Germany.
Height 27.5cm (11in).
Weight 1–3kg (3–7lb).
Coat Long, straight and harsh.
Colour All colours permissible.
Longevity 15 years.
Character Robust, lively, affectionate.

PEKINGESE

Believed to be a relative of the Lhasa Apso and the Shih Tzu, the Pekingese were kept in their thousands in privileged circumstances by the Chinese Imperial court. Five of these dogs were brought to Britain following the Boxer Rebellion in 1860.

Origin China.
Height 15–23cm (6–9in).
Weight 5.0–5.5kg (11–12lb).
Coat Long, straight, coarse, profuse.
Colour All colours permissible.
Longevity 15 years.
Character Dignified, intelligent, fearless.

| 1 | 1 | 3 | 1 |

CHIHUAHUA

The Chihuahua is the smallest dog in the world, and is named after the state of Chihuahua, in Mexico. There are two varieties, the Long-coated (pictured) and Smooth-coated. The practice of interbreeding is no longer allowed.

Origin Mexico.
Height 16–20cm (6–8in).
Weight Up to 3kg (6lb).
Coat Long coat. Long, soft. Smooth coat. Short, dense soft.
Colour All colours permissible.
Longevity 12–14 years.
Character Intelligent, affectionate, possessive.

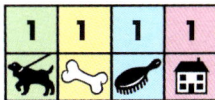

| 1 | 1 | 1 | 1 |

ENGLISH TOY TERRIER

Bred from the Manchester Terrier with blood from the Italian Greyhound and possibly the Whippet, the English Toy terrier has gone through several name changes. They are excellent ratters like the Manchester Terrier.

Origin Great Britain.
Height 25–30cm (10–12in).
Weight 2–4kg (6–9lb).
Coat Thick, close and glossy.
Colour Black and tan.
Longevity 12–13 years.
Character Intelligent, affectionate, one person dog.

2	1	1	1

KING CHARLES SPANIEL

Smaller than the Cavalier King Charles, the King Charles Spaniel became popular when the fashion for short nosed dogs came about. There is still a law in England which enables a King Charles Spaniel 'to go anywhere'.

Origin Japan.
Height 25cm (10in).
Weight 3–7kg (8–14lb).
Coat Long, silky straight coat.
Colour Black and tan, ruby, Blenheim, tricolour.
Longevity 12 years.
Character Full of fun, delightful pet, adaptable.

2	2	2	1

TOY BREEDS

ITALIAN GREYHOUND

An obvious descendant of the Greyhound, the little Italian has been around for a very long time. It is a house-loving family pet which enjoys plenty of exercise. It feels the cold and always needs a coat in chill weather.

Origin Italy.
Height 32–38cm (12–15in).
Weight 2–5kg (5–10lb).
Coat Short, fine and glossy.
Colour Solid black, blue, cream, fawn, red or white.
Longevity 13–14 years.
Character Delightful, affectionate, sensitive.

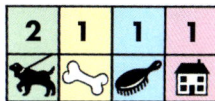

2 1 1 1

MINIATURE PINSCHER

The 'Min Pin' is a delightful high stepping natural showman and a joy to watch. It is descended from the German Pinscher with Italian Greyhound. It has however got a mind of its own and inclined to yap if unchecked.

Origin Germany.
Height 25–30cm (10–12in).
Weight 4.5kg (10lb).
Coat Hard, smooth, short coat.
Colour Black, blue or chocolate with tan.
Longevity 13–14 years.
Character Fearless, self possessed, intelligent.

2 1 1 1

Index

Afghan Hound 44
Airedale Terrier 51
American Cocker Spaniel 38

Basenji 44
Basic care 13, 15
Bassett Hound 46
Bassett Griffon Vendéen 47
Beagle 15, 46
Bearded Collie 30
Bed and bedding 11
Belgian Shepherd Dog 34
Bernese Mountain Dog 26
Bichon Frise 23
Bloodhound 45
Border Collie 31
Border Terrier 53
Borzoi 45
Boston Terrier 18
Boxer 24
Briard 33
Brussels Griffon 58
Bulldog 18
Bullmastiff 29
Bull Terrier 50

Cairn Terrier 53
Canidae 8
Canis familiaris 8
Chihuahua 61
Choosing a dog 10
Chow Chow 14, 21
Clumber Spaniel 38

Dachshund 48
Dalmation 19
Dandie Dinmont Terrier 57
Diet 12
Doberman 25
Dog food 12

Early ancestors 8
English Cocker Spaniel 39
English Foxhound 47
English Setter 42

English Springer Spaniel 39
English Toy Terrier 62

Finnish Spitz 20
Flat Coated Retriever 37
Fox Terrier 51
French Bulldog 19

German Shepherd Dog 14, 34
Golden Retriever 14, 36
Gordon Setter 41
Great Dane 25
Greyhound 48
Grooming 13
Gundogs 14, 36–42

Herding breeds 14, 30–34
Hounds 15, 44–48
Hungarian Puli 35

Indoor kennels 11
Irish Red & White Setter 41
Irish Setter 40
Irish Water Spaniel 37
Irish Wolfhound 49
Italian Greyhound 63

Jack Russell Terrier 52
Japanese Akita 26

Kerry Blue Terrier 52
King Charles Spaniel 62

Lhasa Apso 21
Labrador Retriever 36

Maltese 58
Manchester Terrier 56
Mastiff 29
Miacis 8
Miniature Pinscher 63
Münsterländer 43

Newfoundland 30
Norfolk Terrier 54

Norwich Terrier 54
Nutritional science 12

Old English Sheepdog 32

Papillon 60
Pekingese 61
Picardy Shepherd Dog 35
Pointer 42
Pomeranian 15, 60
Poodle 23
Preparing for a new pet 10
Pug 59
Pyrenean Mountain Dog 27

Rottweiler 14, 24
Rough Collie 32
Routine checks 13

St Bernard 27
Samoyed 28
Scottish Terrier 55
Schnauzer 20
Sealyham Terrier 57
Shar-Pei 22
Shetland Sheepdog 31
Shih Tzu 22
Siberian Husky 28
Skye Terrier 56
Staffordshire Bull Terrier 50

Terriers 15, 50–56
Toy breeds 15, 58–63

Utility breeds 14, 18–22

Weimeraner 43
Welsh Corgi 33
Welsh Springer Spaniel 40
West Highland White Terrier 55
Whippet 49
Wolves 9
Working breeds 14, 24–28

Yorkshire Terrier 15, 59

I N D E X